Turn Loose of Your "But" and Go With God

Letting Go of the Excuses That Are Keeping You From Becoming All God Wants You To Be

by
Eastman Curtis

Harrison House
Tulsa, Oklahoma

*Turn Loose of Your "But" and Go With God:
Letting Go of the Excuses
That Are Keeping You From Becoming
All God Wants You To Be*
ISBN 089274-989-X
Copyright © 1996 by Eastman Curtis
P. O. Box 470290
Tulsa, Oklahoma 74147

Illustrations are by Cory Edwards.

Published by Harrison House, Inc.
P. O. Box 35035
Tulsa, Oklahoma 74153

Contents

Introduction: Letting Go of the Three "Buts"

Then He [Jesus] said to him, "A certain man gave a great supper and invited many,

"and sent his servant at supper time to say to those who were invited, 'Come, for all things are now ready.'

"But they all with one accord *began to make excuses.* The first said to him, 'I have bought a piece of ground, and I must go and see it. I ask you to have me excused.'

"And another said, 'I have bought five yoke of oxen, and I am going to test them. I ask you to have me excused.'

"Still another said, 'I have married a wife, and therefore I cannot come.'

"So that servant came and reported these things to his master. Then the master of the house, being angry, said to the servant, 'Go out quickly into the streets and lanes of the city, and bring in here the poor and the maimed and the lame and the blind.'

"And the servant said, 'Master, it is done as you commanded, and still there is room.'

"Then the master said to his servant, 'Go out into the highways and hedges, and compel them to come in, that my house may be filled.

'For I say to you that none of those men who were invited shall taste my supper.'"

Luke 14:16-24 NKJV

When I read this passage in the Bible, I knew that Jesus was sharing about something more than just going out into the highways and the hedges and commanding or compelling reprobates and the heathen and those who have never heard the Gospel to come in.

So I began to check it out. As part of my study, I looked up that word "supper" in the Greek and found that one of its definitions is "expense."[1]

Just think about it. God has an unlimited treasury of divine expenses for each one of us.

But there are a lot of people who have accepted Jesus Christ as their Savior who have never really tapped into God's "divine expense."

I've come to realize that God doesn't dole out barely enough for you to get by in life, but supersedes even your wildest imagination making sure that all your needs are met. Don't be fooled into thinking that God is standing up there in heaven and rationing His blessings out to us with an eye-dropper as so not to bankrupt heaven. No — He is El Shaddai, the God Who gives more than enough. He desires us to dive into His blessings! I want everything that God has to give. Why? Because Jesus said, "Freely you have received, freely give." (Matthew 1:8 NKJV.)

What I am saying is that there are some "divine expenses" that God has for the believer that many people haven't yet tapped into. Notice that one reason the folks in this story didn't tap into the blessings that were being offered to them was because they began to *make excuses.*

One guy said, "Please excuse me, I just bought a piece of land and have got to go check it out."

Another said, "Please excuse me, I've got to test drive my new ride. You know, I've got twelve oxen-power under the hood, so I wanta crank 'em up and let 'em go!"

The third one said, "I've married a wife, so I can't come." He didn't even ask to be excused, he just said, "No way, man; I just tied the knot, so I ain't comin'!"

Think about how many times we may have made excuses to God: "Lord, I'd love to do such and such, but I can't really do it right now, because of this or because of that."

It's easy to make those great New Year's resolutions: "Lord, I know my body is the temple of the Holy Spirit, and so I'm gonna start an exercise program this year. I know You've been dealing with me about it, and I'm really gonna get started..." Then we think about it a little bit longer, and we add, "...*but*, Lord, I just don't know when I'll have time to do it."

My fifth grade English teacher told me something I've never forgotten. She said, *"Whenever you see that word "but" in a sentence, you can forget whatever comes before it."*

"I want to start that exercise program but..."

How many times has a "but" gotten in the way of your exercise program?

If you are like most people, there's a huge "but" right there in the middle of your good intentions preventing you from doing what you know is best for you and the people around you.

That's what this book is all about — turning loose of the "buts," the excuses, that are keeping us from receiving and enjoying all that God has for us.

What we are going to do in these pages is learn how to dive into God's "divine expenses." After all, isn't that what you really want? It's time to step into a new realm, a new dimension in what God has for you? Aren't you ready to "get with the program"?

Well, in order to do that, you have got to expose and turn loose of the "buts" that are holding you back.

So let's get started!

Endnote

[1] James Strong, "Greek Dictionary of the New Testament," in *Strong's Exhaustive Concordance of the Bible* (Nashville: Abingdon, 1890), p. 21, #1173 "from the same as 1160."

"But" No. 1:
FEAR

On the other hand, a considerable number from the ranks of the leaders did believe. But because of the Pharisees, they didn't come out in the open with it. They were afraid of getting kicked out of the meeting place. When push came to shove they cared more for human approval than for God's glory.

John 12:42,43 THE MESSAGE

Notice that even though this passage says that these people believed on the Lord Jesus Christ, it has that huge word *"but"* in it.

Now I have heard a lot of people say, "Well, if you just believe, that's all that matters."

That's not so. The Bible says in Romans 10:9 that you have to believe in your heart and then CONFESS WITH YOUR MOUTH in order to be saved.

If we aren't ashamed to stand up for Jesus among the people we meet, He will stand up for us before all God's angels. But if we pretend we don't know Him, don't think He will defend us before God's angels. (Luke 12:8,9.)

These people were ready to step over the line. They were just about to enter into God's best for them. But they didn't. Why not? Because "they cared more for human approval than for God's glory."

So if we are going to enter into the blessing of God, the first "but" that has to be exposed and overcome is fear — fear of being rejected by other people.

When we make a decision to serve God, there are going to be some folks who will make fun of us. Once we step over that line, they will call us all sorts of things.

When I first got saved and got turned on to the things of God, people called me preacher man, Bible thumper, chandelier swinger. But I noticed that the ones who laughed at me and ridiculed me the most were the first ones to seek me out when they needed a miracle. When they got into trouble, who do you think they called? That's right, the preacher man, the Bible thumper, the old chandelier swinger, the guy who made a decision to taste and partake of all of God he can possibly get.

Never be afraid of what other people think of you or say about you. Don't fear them, love them. It's the most powerful thing you can do. Let me give you an example.

The Power of Love

Since the time that state-sponsored or state-organized prayer in public schools was outlawed, we have learned a lot about spiritual warfare: how to stand up for what we believe — not to be obnoxious, but to be as wise as serpents and as gentle as doves. (Matthew 10:16.) By that I mean to smile at people, then get out "the Gospel gun," point it at them and "let 'em have it!"

A famous professing atheist was asked to speak at one of our state universities. It was a mandatory assembly, so in the audience there were freshmen, sophomores, juniors and seniors. This person walked out on the platform in front of that huge crowd and began to ridicule and blaspheme and inject doubt, trying to convince the assembly that there is no God, no Jesus, no salvation. At one point, the person even waved a finger in the air and said, "If there really is a God, I want Him to strike me dead right now!"

When I first heard this story, I thought, *Wow, that person is treading on dangerous ground!* God is real, Jesus is alive and sooner or later this person is going to bow down and confess, "Jesus is Lord!" (Philippians 2:10,11).

The reason a lightning bolt didn't come from heaven and turn the atheist into a burnt offering is because God loves the person and didn't want them to perish. Jesus died for atheists, agnostics and all sinners. He loves us all so much and wants to give us as many opportunities as possible to get saved and escape eternal damnation.

Stand Up for Jesus!

After the atheist had made the case against the existence of God in front of those thousands of students, the atheist stepped down from that platform and yelled out, "Now I dare anybody to speak about their God!"

It was deathly quiet in that auditorium. Every person in that audience had been affected. People were just sitting and pondering the words of doubt and unbelief. For about thirty seconds, no one even moved.

Then, in the back of the room, a young girl rose to her feet. The entire time the ungodly person had been ranting and railing against God, a fire had begun to burn in the heart of a little freshman girl who was sitting in the back of the auditorium. As much as she wanted just to be quiet and blend into the crowd, her love for God was stronger than her fear of man. Suddenly it didn't matter any more what people might think of her.

After a few moments of silence, she rose to her feet, took a deep breath and began to sing that old chorus, "Stand up, stand up for Jesus, Ye soldiers of the cross; Lift high his royal banner, It must not suffer loss."

As she continued to sing, in a few moments a few friends sitting next to her rose to their feet and joined in. Then the next row joined, then the next section, and the next section, and then the balcony. Before she had finished singing that old hymn of faith, the entire assembly had risen to their feet and were singing, "Stand up, stand up for Jesus!"

God turned this potentially bad situation around because one girl in that crowd wasn't afraid of what others might think. The same thing can happen in your school if one person isn't ashamed to walk down the hallway of your school with Jesus burning in their heart for everyone to see, not worried about what people think or say — somebody who wants to make a difference. If we are going to enter into the full blessings of God, we have to turn loose of that "but" of the fear of man.

Don't be afraid of what others think or say or do. Stand up, stand up for Jesus!

"FIGHT! FIGHT!"

A while ago my wife and I were ministering in Rochester, New York, where I was asked to speak in a secular college. Whenever I get a chance to speak in a public college or university I always take that opportunity. I figure that if the atheists can speak there, then, glory to God, we believers have a right to equal time!

There was a Christian club on campus, and so I was asked to come and minister. When I walked inside the chapel where the meeting was supposed to be held, I had two guys with me. They were the 1978 and 1979 world champion tag-team kickboxers. Now tag-team kickboxing has been outlawed because too many people were getting hurt.

These two former kickboxers had gotten saved and filled with the Holy Ghost through our ministry. They travel with us occasionally, and we always have a blast. They just happened to be with me on this trip to Rochester.

As we walked into that meeting, I noticed that there were about three people in the congregation. There was one guy sitting there with an acoustic guitar, strumming along and quietly singing "Kum-ba-ya." I looked around at the walls, and there were signs everywhere welcoming Eastman Curtis to the campus — and only three people had showed up to hear me! They were there with their Bibles open, all excited about hearing the Gospel.

Now when I hold a meeting at a secular college, I am really wanting "non-Christians" to come. Since this was not a Christian school, I knew there had to be unbelievers everywhere. So I called my two kickboxer friends over and said to them, "Come on, I've got a plan."

I turned to the guy playing the guitar and told him, "Just go ahead and make your announcements right now. I'm gonna go get a crowd."

I walked over to the cafeteria, which was just cram-packed with humanity. I stood on a chair and yelled, "Hey, can I have your attention, please? Attention, attention! Ladies and gentleman, for today and today only, we have with us the 1978-79 world champion kickboxers!"

Everyone in the place started screaming, "Yeahhh!"

"They are about to put on an exhibition you won't want to miss," I said, "It's right over there in the auditorium. Follow me."

As I was leaving, I looked behind me at my two friends, and their eyes were bugging out.

"What're we doing?" they wanted to know.

I looked behind them, and I saw that there were at least 150 people following us. I felt like the pied piper.

So we all piled into the chapel. I left the doors open, cranked up the P.A. system, duct-taped the volume controls to ten, and started yelling into the mike, "Okay, gang, let's have church!"

Now these two friends of mine hadn't practiced kickboxing in years. They weren't even warmed up. But since I had put them on the spot, they just started beating the mess out of each other. While they were doing that, and people were filling up the place, I started yelling, "FIGHT! FIGHT! THERE'S A FIGHT IN HERE!"

You know, a fight will draw a crowd every time. So more people started running from everywhere.

Those two guys went at it for a while. Then when they got done, they took the microphone and said, "I want you to know that Jesus Christ has changed our lives. Now Eastman Curtis is gonna get up there and tell you more about Him."

I got up and preached for five minutes. At the end of that five-minute message, a hundred college students gave their hearts to Jesus Christ!

Just Do It!

If you won't be afraid of what other people think about you, you can change the world. When the Holy Spirit tells you to do something, don't hesitate — just do it.

Of course, you must always be sure that what you're experiencing is a prompting of the Holy Spirit and not just a guilt trip or feelings of condemnation.

How can you tell the difference? It's easy. If it's the Spirit of God, then you will feel good about it. You will feel like saying, "Oh, yeah!" You will have supernatural confidence. Like the psalmist, you will feel like you can run through a troop and leap over a wall. (Psalm 18:29 KJV.) You may even feel like you can leap over a troop and run through a wall! Actually, you can do either.

How can you tell whether a prompting is from the Lord or whether you are just under a spirit of self-obligation? When the Lord prompts you to do something, there is always a sense of joy. It just begins to bubble up on the inside and flow on the outside.

In my own case, when the Holy Spirit has come upon me, I have found myself doing some of the craziest things — in the natural — that I have ever done in my life.

One time I was riding my motorcycle down the street, just worshipping God. As I was singing and praising the Lord, I followed a truck right into a driveway.

"What am I doing here?" I asked myself. Just as I started to turn and leave, from the house I heard people screaming, pots and pans banging and little children crying at the top of their lungs.

When I heard all this commotion, a Holy Ghost boldness hit me. I jumped off that cycle like a Ninja turtle! I went up to the house, threw the door open without even knocking and walked right into the middle of the living room shouting "I'm here in the name of Jesus!"

When I did that, a little man just blew past me — *"whewwwwww"* — right out the front door. Then I saw a woman standing there with her three small children. Her eyes and mouth were wide open. She looked right at me and said, "Young man, I don't know who you are...."

I just sort of hung my head, thinking, "Well, I don't know who I am either. I'm just passing through." All I could think of was getting out of there as quick as I could.

Then the woman went on, "...but, you know, I've been praying that God would send somebody to tell me more about Him."

You see, when we step out in obedience to God, we will become the answer to somebody's prayer.

But if we are going to do that, if we are going to excel in what God has for us, if we are going to be all that the Lord wants us to be, the first thing we must do is turn loose of the "but" of the fear of man.

"But" No. 2:
PROCRASTINATION

He said to Moses: Go to the palace and tell the king of Egypt that I order him to let my people go, so they can worship me.

If he refuses, I will cover his entire country with frogs.

Exodus 8:1,2 THE PROMISE

When I was a little kid, I loved frogs. Today my little boy loves frogs. There are even some women who love frogs. But not my wife. She is petrified of them; she can't stand them.

Not long ago we were opening the door to our house and this big old green-honking tree frog was standing right there in the doorway. Of all the things to do, that frog attacked my wife — he jumped right up into her face and just hung there!

Tree frogs have little suction cups on the bottom of their feet so they can hold onto tree trunks. So there this huge green tree frog was stuck onto my wife's lips. She was running around yelling, "Ahhhh! Get him off, get him off!" Finally, she pulled him free, threw him out the door and ran to soak her lips in Listerine.

 Is it any wonder that she hates frogs?

I believe God chose frogs to send as a curse on the mothers in Egypt because He knew that, as the old saying goes, "When Mama ain't happy, nobody's happy!" When Mama has to soak her lips in Listerine, everybody has to soak their lips in Listerine.

An Abundance of Frogs

Warn the king that the Nile will be full of frogs, and from

there they will spread into the royal palace, including the king's bedroom and even his bed. Frogs will enter the homes of his officials and will find their way into ovens and into the bowls of bread dough.

Frogs will be crawling on everyone-the king, his officials, and every citizen of Egypt.

Exodus 8:3,4 THE PROMISE

Can you just imagine having frogs in your house, on your bed, in your closet, in your bathroom, in your kitchen?

Now that is a lot of frogs!

How would you like to go in to brush your teeth and find a frog hanging on

your toothbrush in the morning? What if you went to the stove to put the pastry in the oven and found it full of frogs? How would you like to open the microwave and discover it hanging with frogs? I mean, you can only do so much with frogs' legs!

That's the curse that the Lord was threatening to place on Pharaoh and his people if they didn't let His people go and serve Him.

"Take Away These Frogs..."

Moses, now command Aaron to hold his stick over the water. Then frogs will come from all rivers, canals, and ponds in Egypt, and they will cover the land.

Aaron obeyed, and suddenly frogs were everywhere in Egypt.

The king sent for Moses and Aaron and told them, "If you ask the Lord to take these frogs away from me and my people, I will let your people go and offer sacrifices to him."

Exodus 8:5,6,8 THE PROMISE

It looked like Moses and Aaron had won a victory. God slapped Pharaoh with the frogs, and he bowed his knee. But as we know, he later recanted.

But for the moment, at least, Pharaoh was tired of the frogs, and so he told Moses to ask the Lord to take them away. But notice when he wanted this done.

"... Tomorrow!"

"All right," Moses answered. "You choose the time when I am to pray for the frogs to stop bothering you, your officials, and your people, and for them to leave your houses and be found only in the river."

"Do it tomorrow!" the king replied.

"As you wish," Moses agreed. "Then everyone will discover that there is no god like the LORD."

Exodus 8:9,10 THE PROMISE

Do you know what that meant? It meant that Pharaoh had to spend one more night with frogs! It meant one more night with frogs in his supper bowl, one more night having frogs hanging from his toothbrush, one more night taking a shower with frogs, one more night to climb into a bed filled with frogs.

Pharaoh had a choice. He was given the honor of choosing when the curse of frogs would end, but instead of saying, "Today,"

he said, "Tomorrow!"

So the second "but" that has to be exposed and removed is the "but" of procrastination, of putting off until later what should be done right now.

A Convenient Time

As Paul continued to insist on right relations with God and his people, about a life of moral discipline and the coming Judgment, Felix felt things getting a little too close for comfort and dismissed him. "That's enough for today. I'll call you back when it's convenient."

Acts 24:25 THE MESSAGE

So often in the Word of God we see people who put off responding to the call of the Lord on their lives, as here in this passage with Felix.

Often we see that kind of thing happening today. The Spirit of the Lord starts wooing, starts dealing with people, starts calling to them, "Come and enter into what God has for you," and their response is: "Yeah, I'll do that...just as soon as I graduate from high school."

Then when they get their diploma, they say, "I'll do that...just as soon as I get out of college."

Then when they get their degree, it becomes "...just as soon as I get married."

Then after the wedding it becomes "...as soon as my kids are raised and out on their own."

Then when the children are grown and gone, it's "...as soon as we retire and have more time."

And then it's too late!

Today's the Day!

Well, now is the right time to listen, the day to be helped.

2 Corinthians 6:2
THE MESSAGE

Behold, now is the accepted time; behold, now is the day of salvation.

2 Corinthians 6:2 KJV

Don't put off until tomorrow what needs to be done today.

"There's always tomorrow" is one of the biggest lies the devil will ever tell you. The Bible doesn't talk about later, it talks about *now* — *now* is the time, *now* is the day of salvation.

Yesterday is gone, and tomorrow never comes.

Today is the day!

Start Moving!

Then the LORD answered me and said:

"Write the vision
And make it plain on tablets,
That *he may run* who reads it.

For the vision is yet for an appointed time...."

Habakkuk 2:2,3 NKJV

God may be speaking to you right now, calling you to do something. He may be speaking to you about becoming self-employed or about moving into a new level of work or about starting a new ministry.

You may be saying, "Okay, sure, I'll do that. Just let me get one more tape series and listen to it, then I'll begin. Just let me go to one more seminar, then after that, I promise I'll really get with it!"

Don't do that. Start where you are today with what you have today! Even if you don't have the final goal clearly in mind, start moving in the right direction now!

It's essential that we begin moving in the right direction as soon as we get the call. The longer we put it off, the more unsure of the voice of the Lord we will become.

Have you ever been praying and heard the Lord speaking to you? Maybe it was a solid ten on the Richter scale. The Lord spoke to you, and you knew it.

But then after you left the prayer closet you began to think, "Now, wait a minute. Maybe I'd better think about this thing for a while."

So you put off doing what the Lord said for you to do for a little while, and then a little while longer, and then a little while longer. And the more you put it off, the more you questioned, "Did God really speak to me about doing that?" You ended up not being sure whether God had spoken to you or not.

Why did that happen? It happened because you procrastinated. As long as you were in the prayer closet, you knew without a doubt that God was speaking to you. But the longer you put off responding to that call, the more unsure of it you became.

That's the danger of procrastination. It produces doubt and uncertainty — which leads to disobedience and failure.

When the Spirit of the Lord instructs you to do something, at least start heading in that direction. The manifestation of the vision may be "for an appointed time." It may point to something down the road, but if you can't reach it at once, at least start down the road toward it.

Don't put it off; "get it in gear."

Don't just stand there; do something.

Don't think about; do it!

Don't wait and see if it will come to pass on its own; take action!

Act On It!

One of my favorite books in the Bible is what everybody calls simply "Acts." Notice that it is not called the book of philosophy, nor the book of thought. It's not even called the book of meditation. No, it's called the book of the *Acts* of the Apostles.

I like that. Why? Because it is the record of people responding to the Word of God — not just mentally assenting to it, but acting on it.

That's what God wants us to do. He doesn't want us to put it off, He wants us to get on it. He wants us to act on what He has called us to do. As we begin to do that, we will begin to see results.

Let me give you an example from everyday life.

Once when I was ministering in upstate New York, there was a nice little grandmother, the kind who makes cookies with icing that says, "Jesus loves you." She was an incredible woman and just as sweet as the icing on her cookies.

Well, one day this sweet little granny was in a grocery store standing at the checkout counter when suddenly she heard someone calling from the meat section: "Man down, man down!"

Everyone rushed to the back of the store where a man was lying on the floor having a heart attack. So Grandma Alice put down her groceries and went back "to see about the poor man."

When she got there, she saw a whole crew of people down on the floor trying to help him. A registered nurse was giving him CPR and mouth to mouth resuscitation. But it didn't seem to be doing any good.

"As I stood there, the Spirit of God spoke to me and told me to do something," Grandma Alice said later. "He told me to pray for that man. All of a sudden it didn't matter to me what those other people might think. I knew I was just going to do it. I was just going to act on what the Spirit of the Lord had said for me to do."

So she walked right into the midst of that crowd, looked at the nurse and told her, "Ma'am, get out of the way."

She said it with such boldness and authority that the nurse moved out of the way. Little Grandma Alice placed her hand on the man's head and said, "In the name of Jesus, man, be whole!"

As soon as she said that, the man sat up and looked around.

"Lie back down, lie back down," the nurse told him. So he lay back down, and

the paramedics came and rushed him off to the hospital where the doctors couldn't find one thing wrong with his heart!

Do you know why? Because God had done a miracle. And He had done it through His handmaiden who was not afraid of other people and who did not waste time procrastinating.

How many blessings do we miss simply because we let fear and procrastination rob us of what God has for us?

Whenever you hear the voice of the Lord telling you to do something, don't put it off. Just do it — and you will see the blessings of the Lord begin to manifest in your life.

"But" No. 3:
INADEQUACY

Then the word of the LORD came to me, saying:

> *"Before I formed you in the womb I knew you;*
>
> *Before you were born I sanctified you;*
>
> I ordained you a prophet to the nations."

Jeremiah 1:4,5 NKJV

When the Lord called Jeremiah as a young man, He told him that He had chosen and anointed him before he was born, before he was even formed in the womb, to fulfill a worldwide ministry.

Let's look at Jeremiah's response to this prompting of the Holy Spirit.

"I Can't Do That!"

Then said I:

"Ah, Lord GOD!

Behold, *I cannot* speak,
for I am a youth."

Jeremiah 1:6 NKJV

When the Lord called Jeremiah as a prophet to the nations, the first thing he did was protest: "Oh, God, I can't do that!"

Do you remember when God called Moses from the burning bush and told him that he was to go and lead the children of Israel out of slavery in the land of Egypt? The first thing Moses said (in so many words) was: "Oh, God, I can't do that! Lord, You've got the wrong guy.

You know I can't speak well. Get my brother Aaron, he can talk much better than I can. I'm a stutterer. I'm just not the man for the job." (Exodus 3,4.)

Then there was Gideon. When the Lord called him to lead His people against the Midianites, his answer was: "Oh, God, I can't do that! I'm a nobody. I'm the least in my family, and my family is the least in Israel." (Judges 6.)

Many times when God gives someone a vision of what He has for him to do, the first thing that person will say is: "Oh, God, I would love to do that, *but* I can't; I'm just not able."

This is the third "but" that has to be exposed and overcome — the "but" of inadequacy.

Jeremiah's excuse was that he was too young to be a world-class prophet. "I can't do that," he said, "I'm just a pup. Why, I'm still wet behind the ears. Wait till I get older, and then we'll see about it."

But notice, the Lord doesn't want to hear any excuses.

"Don't Say That!"

But the LORD said to me:
> "*Do not say*, 'I am a youth,'
> For you shall go to
>   all to whom I send you,
> And whatever I command
>   you, you shall speak.
> "Do not be afraid of their
>   faces,
> For I am with you to
>   deliver you," says the
>   LORD.
>
> Jeremiah 1:7,8 NKJV

Don't make excuses to God. He's not interested in hearing them.

And don't be intimidated by Satan. He's a liar. He will tell you that you are going to fail, that you are going down in defeat, that you are going under. That's a lie! You are not going under, you are going over — because you are an overcomer! (1 John 5:4,5.)

And, finally, don't be intimidated by people. The Lord has commanded, "Do not be afraid of their faces." Why not? Because He has promised to be with you and to deliver you.

"See, I Have Put You Over!"

Then the LORD put forth His hand and touched my mouth, and the LORD said to me:

> "Behold, I have put My words in your mouth.

> *"See, I have this day set you over the nations and over the kingdoms,*

> To root out and to pull down, To destroy and to throw down, To build and to plant."

> Jeremiah 1:9,10 NKJV

When God calls, He equips. With the call goes the power. You just need to step out on that equipping power. Don't hesitate or make excuses or be afraid, just step into what God is calling you to do. And the best way to start is by being faithful with the job He has given you to do right now.

"Yeah, but I want to preach to thousands, I want to minister to millions."

Well then, start where you are. Don't you know that there are lots of people right where you live or go to school or work who need to hear about Jesus?

If you really want to reach people for the Lord all around *His* world, then start by reaching those He has placed all around *your* world.

Start by Being Faithful

He who is faithful in what is *least* is faithful also in *much*.

Luke 16:10

I always wanted to be a preacher. When the Lord called me, I got so excited I could hardly wait to get started preaching. But do you know what I was doing at the time? I was playing the drums in a church in Lakeland, Florida. This church had five services on Sunday, and every single Sunday I would be there, playing drums in each of those five services.

Praise God, I drummed to the glory of the Lord!

I didn't *have* to drum, I *got* to drum.

It was a privilege, an honor, to get to do that. I was so turned on to the Lord that I was willing to do anything to please Him.

I said to the pastor of that church, "Pastor, here I am. I'll do anything you want me to do. I'll even clean toilets."

"Well," he said, "we don't really need any toilet cleaners right now."

I was so eager to get started ministering that I volunteered for anything that would get me into preaching. Although I wanted to be up front preaching, all this time I was faithfully playing drums in the background.

Then one day while one of the regular Sunday school teachers was on vacation, the pastor called and said, "Eastman, I need you to teach a college and career class. Will you do it?"

"Yeah, I'll do it!" I said.

On the outside I was "ready and willing," but on the inside I was "shakin' in my boots." The spirit was willing, but the flesh was weak! My big chance had finally come, and I was feeling inadequate.

So I got started preparing for that class. I studied, I prayed, I paced back and forth across the floor, I spoke in tongues, I did it all. I had that message just burning my heart.

When I got in front of that class, I just stood up tall and "let 'er rip"! I blasted through five pages of notes in three minutes. I didn't know what to do then, so I gave an altar call — in Sunday school!

There were about 110 college students in that class, and when the altar call was made ten of them gave their hearts to Jesus Christ.

Then I prayed for the baptism in the Holy Spirit, and twenty-three of them were baptized in the Spirit and spoke in tongues.

I just kept ministering. I was faithful.

After a while, I was asked to teach Sunday school full time. Then my messages got a little bit longer. I began to feel more comfortable standing in front of an audience and ministering.

Finally, someone asked me, "Eastman, would you like to come minister at my church? We're having a camp, would you like to speak?"

"Yeah, I'll do it!"

Again, on the outside I was ready and willing. But on the inside I was thinking, "With my own people I feel comfortable. They know me. I don't have to prove myself to them. But this is a brand new bunch of folks, people I've never even seen before."

But I convinced myself to do it. I just acted on the leading of the Spirit — and the Lord moved mightily.

When somebody else asked me to speak, I agreed. Then someone else asked me to speak, and then someone else, and the next thing I knew I was walking in the call of the Lord for my life.

Now God didn't grab me by the arm, jerk me up and say, "Okay, boy, I've called you to be a preacher, so go get 'em!" No, He led me step by step, and He taught me precept by precept.

Do you remember when God spoke to the children of Israel before they entered Canaan to take possession of the land He had promised them? He told them, "I'm going to lead you into a land that flows with milk and honey. But I'm not going to give it to you all at once. You're going to have to take it city by city, piece by piece, lest the land devour you." (Exodus 23:27-31, author's paraphrase.)

That's what God wants to do for you and me.

If you want to be master over much, start by being faithful in what is least. Begin by heading in the right direction, and the Lord will lead your steps. Don't keep putting it off. Don't procrastinate. Step into what the Lord has for you. And don't give into feelings of inadequacy. Be assured that God has equipped you for the work He has called you to do.

Whom God Calls, He Equips

Many times we come to God feeling so inadequate. Part of the problem is that we listen to the devil who is a master at inadequacy.

The Lord has revealed to me that you want so much to be of service to Him. Like me, on the outside you are "chompin' at the bit" to be used by the Lord, but on the inside you feel so inadequate. Like Jeremiah and Moses and Gideon, you keep saying, "Oh, God, I can't do that!" But remember, when the Lord calls a person, He always equips him to fulfill that call.

God equipped Jeremiah and Moses and Gideon to do the work that He placed in their hearts to do. And He will do the same for you. He *wants* you to step out in your calling and to dwell in it.

"When Will I Be Adequate Enough?"

When I was saved and filled with the Holy Ghost, I was sitting in the back of the church because I had got there late. The pastor gave an altar call, and I saw two of my best friends go down to the front to receive Jesus.

These two guys had been buddies of mine since high school when we used to party together. When I saw them go forward to make Jesus Lord of their lives and be welcomed into the family of God, I jumped out of my seat and headed toward the front too.

As I started down the aisle, I suddenly began to feel inadequate. I started thinking, "God, I can't do this. I mean, what's gonna happen if the pastor starts askin' me questions I don't know the answer to?"

Do you know what was the first question the devil told me I was going to be asked? The dimensions of the Ark of the Covenant!

Isn't that the dumbest thing you ever heard? My buddies were down front getting saved, and they didn't know the dimensions of the Ark of the Covenant. But the devil kept whispering in my ear, "What if the pastor asks you that question? What are you going to say?"

I felt so inadequate that as I was walking down the aisle to receive the Lord I was busy flipping through my Thomas Chain Bible trying to find the dimensions to the Ark of the Covenant! I couldn't find it, so I slid into a pew, buried my face in my hands and began to cry, "Oh, God, when will I ever be good enough, when will I ever be adequate enough?"

That night the Holy Spirit showed me something that transformed my life. It was there in the Bible all along, but somehow I had missed it. I don't want you to miss it, because it is so simple and so beautiful.

"Our Sufficiency Is From God"

Not that we are sufficient of ourselves to think of anything as being from ourselves, *but our sufficiency is from God.*

2 Corinthians 3:5 NKJV

Now when most people read this verse, they stop after the first part, "Not that we are sufficient of ourselves..."

The devil will say: "That's true. You're so inadequate. You know the dream you have in your heart is too big for your ability. You know you don't have the talent or the personality or the education to fulfill it. You can't do it, you're not good enough, you're just not sufficient."

Yes, the Bible does say that we are not sufficient in ourselves, but notice that this statement is followed by the word "*but*"! This time, it is not our "but," it is God's. And that makes all the difference in the world!

Read the second part of that verse again: "...but our sufficiency is from God."

Where does our sufficiency, our adequacy, our competence come from? It comes not from us, *but* from God. It is not our sufficiency, our adequacy, our competence that matters: it is God's sufficiency, God's adequacy, God's competence flowing through us.

Too often we come to God all cowered down, thinking that we are just "poor old sinners saved by grace."

No, we are not "poor old sinners." We *were* "poor old sinners," but not any more! Now we have been made the righteousness of God in Christ. (2 Corinthians 5:21.) Now we can stand before God faultless, without guilt or condemnation, without a sense of inferiority or inadequacy. Because now we are children of God — and our heavenly Father loves us.

Come Boldly to the Throne

Let us therefore come *boldly* to the throne of grace, that we may obtain mercy and find grace to help in time of need.

Hebrews 4:16 NKJV

When I was little, my father would come home from work every day about five-thirty, just about the time the Flintstones cartoons were over. When I heard the closing theme song, I knew it was time for Dad to arrive, so I would jump up and run to the window to watch for him.

I loved my father so much. When he would drive up, I would be standing there with my face pressed against the window glass.

Every now and then he would bring me a Butterfinger candy bar. (I liked them before Bart Simpson was even conceived!) So I would be watching as Dad got out of the car, and if he had a Butterfinger for me I could tell because I could see that bright yellow wrapper with the blue writing on it sticking out of his pocket.

I would get so excited, I would start yelling, "Dad's home! Dad's home! And he's got a Butterfinger!" Then I would run and hide behind the couch.

Dad would open the door and holler, "I'm home!"

"Dada!" I would yell, and run to tackle him. We would climb up onto the big old recliner, and I would start going through his pockets looking for that Butterfinger. As soon as I found it, I would shove the whole thing in my mouth, and crumbs would start flying everywhere.

Some of the fondest memories of my life are those moments we spent together as I sat with my head up against Dad's chest, happily munching away on a Butterfinger. I loved it, and I loved my father for doing it for me. And he loved doing it.

Now what would have happened if Dad had come home from work, and I was hiding behind the couch — not because I was excited and wanted to jump out and tackle him for that candy bar, but because I felt ashamed and afraid and unworthy to approach him.

How would Dad have felt if I had crawled out on my hands and knees, crying pitifully, "Oh, my father, I perceive that there is a Butterfinger in thy pocket. Oh father, I am so unworthy. If I could but gaze upon it for a season! Oh, if I could but sniff the wrapper!"

If I had done that, my dad would probably have grabbed me up and shook me like a rag doll, saying, "Look, son, what's wrong with you? I brought you this candy bar because I love you, and I want you to have it. Now quit acting like a low-down dog!"

Yet, many times that is how we approach God in prayer. We come crawling up to our Father's "recliner," His throne of grace, with our tail between our legs, weeping and wailing, squalling and bawling, acting like we don't deserve to be there.

You don't have to do that. You are a child of God, He is your loving Father. You can come *boldly* to His throne to receive from Him whatever you need — without any sense of guilt or condemnation or inadequacy.

It's God's Righteousness, Not Our Righteousness

For they being ignorant of God's righteousness, and *seeking to establish their own righteousness*, have not submitted to the righteousness of God.

Romans 10:3 NKJV

Too often we try to earn our salvation, our righteousness, our holiness, our right standing with God. That is a mistake.

I want you to know that when God looks at one of us, He doesn't say, "Wow, now that's one righteous dude! But, man, that guy over there, he barely got saved."

No, we are all saved by the same plan of redemption. When God looks at us, He doesn't care whether we have been saved for four days or for forty years. One of us is just as righteous in His eyes as the other. Why? Because we are all saved by the blood of Jesus, not by our own merits. When we were saved, we received the righteousness of Christ, which is the same for each of us.

When God looks at us, He doesn't see our righteousness, He sees the righteousness of His Son Jesus Christ — and that is sufficient. We don't have to earn our Father's affection, or His approval or His acceptance.

Accepted in the Beloved

Blessed be the God and Father of our Lord Jesus Christ, who has blessed us with every spiritual blessing in the heavenly places in Christ, just as He chose us in Him before the foundation of the world, that we should be holy and without blame before Him in love,

having predestined us to adoption as sons by Jesus Christ to Himself, according to the good pleasure of His will,

to the praise of the glory of His grace, by which *He made us accepted in the Beloved.*

Ephesians 1:3-6 NKJV

I loved my father, but he was not perfect. Although I tried my best, I could never quite get his full approval.

Now my little sister made straight A's in school with no sweat. She never even brought a book home. But good grades didn't come that easy for me. I had to work for them. I would study like crazy, pulling my hair out, tape recording everything, playing it over and over in my head all night long. The next morning when I woke up I couldn't remember a thing I had studied.

I worked hard in school, but no matter how hard I worked or how good my grades were, when I would proudly bring home my report card, Dad would always ignore all the A's on it and focus on the one B I had made.

"Son, that's pretty good," he would say, "but you need to bring that B up."

"But Dad, I tried so hard!"

"I know you did, son, but you can do better than that."

The same thing happened in sports. For years I tried something called "punt, pass and kick." This was a kind of individual competition between kids in a certain age bracket to see which one could punt, pass and kick a football the farthest. I practiced and practiced and finally managed to win a gold award. I was

so proud of it, I took it home to show it
to my father.

"Look what I won, Dad!"

"Son, that's great. What's it for?"

"Punt, pass and kick."

"How far did you punt the ball?"

I told him.

"How far did you throw it?"

I told him.

"How far did you kick it?

I told him.

He just hung his head and said, "I've
seen you play, son, and you can do better
than that."

I wanted so much for my father to
accept me, but it seemed that no matter
how hard I tried, no matter what I
accomplished, it was never enough to win
his approval.

Well, after he got saved, he understood better, and the Lord has since restored those years that the locusts devoured. (Joel 2:25.)

But if we are not careful, we will transfer that kind of approval-seeking to our relationship with our heavenly Father. We will begin to try to win His acceptance by our good works.

"Look, Father, I led three people to Christ today. Isn't that great?"

"Look, Father, I prayed for five people today, and they were filled with the Holy Ghost and spoke in tongues. Isn't that great?"

"Look, Father, I read fifteen chapters in the Bible today. Of course, I don't remember what I read — but isn't that great?"

"Look, Father, I prayed a whole hour today? Am I accepted now?"

We don't have to do all that to be accepted by God. The Bible says that because of His great love for us, we are already accepted in the Beloved.

We don't have to earn God's acceptance. We don't have to pray in tongues or work miracles or do exploits to be accepted by our heavenly Father. We were accepted by Him when we received His Son Jesus Christ as our Savior and Lord.

Saved for Good Works, Not by Good Works

For *by grace you have been saved* through faith, and that not of yourselves; it is the gift of God,

not of works, lest anyone should boast.

For we are His workmanship, created in Christ Jesus *for* good works, which God prepared beforehand that we should walk in them.

Ephesians 2:8-10 NKJV

Notice that this passage makes it clear that it is by God's *grace* that we are saved and not by our *works*.

It also makes it clear that we are not saved *by* good works but *for* good works. That is a big difference.

Yet so often we still try to earn our salvation — after we have already freely received it by grace through faith.

"Oh, God, I am doing all these things because I just want You to be pleased with me."

Yet the Bible says that we are already accepted in the Beloved; that is, in Christ Jesus.

Does that mean that we are not to share the Good News of Jesus with others? Does it mean that we are not to read the Word of God, or pray, or worship with others in God's house?

No, it just means that we are not to do all this because God is standing over us with a big two-by-four in His hands saying, "If you want to be accepted, you'd better do these things!"

That's not God. It's not the way He wants us to see Him ourselves, and it's not the way He wants us to present Him to others.

The Bible says that it was because God so loved the world that He gave His only begotten Son Jesus Christ so that the whole world might have eternal and abundant life. (John 3:16; John 10:10.) Because God loves the world, He wants us to love it too. Because He loves us, all of us, each of us, He wants us to love one another and share with one another — freely.

Freely Received,
Freely Given

...Freely you have received, *freely* give.

Matthew 10:8 NKJV

Our heavenly Father has freely given us peace and joy and many other wonderful blessings. Now He wants us to share those marvelous blessings with others. Not because we have to, but because we want to. Not because we want to win God's approval, but because we want others to "taste and see that the Lord is good" (Psalm 34:8), just as we have done.

Once we have done that, once we have truly come to know the Lord and His goodness and love, ministry becomes not a "have-to" but a "want-to."

We don't *have to* share the Gospel with others, we *want to* tell them how wonderful God is and what He has done for us.

We don't *have to* pray for people to be saved or baptized in the Holy Spirit, we *want to* see them come to know the Lord and to enter into the fullness of His power.

We don't *have to* pray for people to be healed, we *want to* see them restored to health.

We don't *have to* cast demons out of people, we *want to* see them set free from the power of the evil one.

We don't *have to* read God's Word, we *get to* read God's Word. And when we do, we don't do it to be accepted; no, we do it because we already are accepted. We read the Word of God so we can get to know Him better and love and serve Him better.

We don't pray because we *have to* put in so many hours a week, but because we *want to* be in constant communion with your heavenly Father.

Just think about it, we get to have a personal, private conversation with the Creator of the universe! We can climb up into the lap of the One Who spoke the worlds into existence and call him Father, Abba, Daddy! We are His children, and He loves us!

Prayer

If you are serious about living fearlessly for God, being a doer of His Word and not a hearer only, allowing nothing to hold you back from fulfilling His call on your life and enjoying his blessings to the full, then pray this simple prayer right now:

"Father, I thank You for Your Son Jesus Christ Who died for me that I might have life everlasting and life in all its abundance.

"Thank You, Lord, for calling me to know You and to bring others to know You too.

"Thank You for all the blessings that You have poured out upon me. Freely I have received, freely I will share with those around me.

"Thank You for Your Holy Spirit to guide me in my daily walk. With His help I never allow fear of others, or my own procrastination or feelings of adequacy, to keep me from fulfilling Your perfect plan and purpose for my life.

"In Jesus' name, I pray. Amen."

Bible References

Scriptures quotations marked KJV are taken from the *King James Version* of the Bible.

Scripture quotations marked NKJV are taken from *The New King James Version of the Bible*. Copyright © 1979, 1980, 1982, Thomas Nelson, Inc.

Scriptures quotations marked THE MESSAGE are taken from *The Message: New Testament With Psalms and Proverbs* by Eugene H. Peterson. Copyright © 1993, 1994, 1995 by Eugene H. Peterson. NavPress, P. O. Box 35001, Colorado Springs, Colorado 80935.

Scripture quotations marked THE PROMISE are taken from *The Promise®, Contemporary English Version*. Copyright © 1995, Thomas Nelson, Inc.

About the Author

Although **Eastman Curtis** was raised in an influential family in central Florida, by the age of 16 he had been expelled from three schools for drug and alcohol use. When Eastman turned 17, he had a powerful experience with Jesus that drastically altered the rest of his life. His dramatic conversion and radical transformation caused a revival to explode on his high school campus. Eastman personally saw over 100 students receive Christ as their Savior that year!

As God's power began to saturate every area of his life, Eastman went from a flunky to an honor student and senior class president. He received a college scholarship for his leadership capabilities and exemplary conduct, the first of its kind awarded to anyone at his college preparatory school. Eastman's family could not believe the difference, and today, his entire family has been saved as a result of the supernatural change in his life.

Eastman travels the world preaching in churches and holding crusades, challenging teenagers and adults to catch a vision for God. Formerly the host of the TV show *"This Generation,"* Eastman has launched into new areas by conducting *"This Generation Youth Conventions"* as well as putting his new television special, *"Eastman Curtis Live,"* on secular networks such as FOX and WGN. He is recognized as one of the most powerful youth speakers in America and had the honor of fulfilling his duties as the National Director of Prayer for *Washington for Jesus*. His contagious joy and encouragement are always refreshing. His messages; whether in person, on video or in books; will inspire you to go full force for God's best in your life.

To contact the author, write:

Eastman Curtis • P. O. Box 470290
Tulsa, Oklahoma 74147

Additional copies of this book are available
from your local bookstore.

Harrison House
Tulsa, Oklahoma 74153

In Canada contact:

Word Alive • P. O. Box 670
Niverville, Manitoba • CANADA R0A 1E0